# BUTTON UP!

# BUTTON UP!

Wrinkled Rhymes by Alice Schertle

Pictures by Petra Mathers

sandpiper

HOUGHTON MIFFLIN HARCOURT

BOSTON NEW YORK

To Spence, Dylan, Jen, Drew, Kate, and John: Don't forget your jackets —A.S.
For Ruby, Oscar, and Ezra, at night in their jammies —P.M.

Text copyright © 2009 by Alice Schertle
Illustrations copyright © 2009 by Petra Mathers

All rights reserved. Published in the United States by Sandpiper, an imprint of
Houghton Mifflin Harcourt Publishing Company. Originally published in hard-
cover in the United States by Harcourt Children's Books, an imprint of Houghton
Mifflin Harcourt Publishing Company, 2009.

SANDPIPER and the SANDPIPER logo are trademarks of Houghton Mifflin Harcourt
Publishing Company.

For information about permission to reproduce selections from this book, write to
trade.permissions@hmhco.com or to Permissions, Houghton Mifflin Harcourt
Publishing Company, 3 Park Avenue, 19th Floor, New York, New York 10016.

www.hmhco.com

The illustrations in this book were done in watercolor
on Arches 300 lb. cold-press paper.
The display type was set in Kosmik Bold One.
The text type was set in Kosmik Plain One.
Designed by Jennifer Jackman and Michele Wetherbee

The Library of Congress has cataloged the hardcover edition as follows:
Schertle, Alice.
Button up/Alice Schertle; illustrations by Petra Mathers.
p. cm.
1. Children's clothing—Poetry. I. Mathers, Petra, ill. II. Title.
PS3569.C48435B88  2009
811.54-dc22  2007042839

ISBN: 978-0-15-205050-4 hardcover
ISBN: 978-0-544-02269-0 paperback

Manufactured in China
SCP 10 9 8

4500710280

# CONTENTS

# Bertie's
## SHOELACES

Good old Bertie,
he lets us hang around.
It doesn't bother Bertie
when we drag along the ground.
We're not up tight
as our Bertie buddy knows.
We're hang loose laces and
*we don't do bows!*

# Violet's **HIKING HAT**

I am Violet's hiking hat.
I live on Violet's head.
"I NEVER take off my hiking hat,"
Violet said.

I'm taking a hike with Violet.
Violet's showing me things.
"Hat," says Violet, "there's a caboose.
These are butterfly wings."

"Hat," says Violet, "here's a rock.
These are the monkey bars."
Violet takes me out at night.
"Look," says Violet. "Stars."

Here in the bathtub with Violet
we're having a storm at sea—
a whale, a rabbit, a submarine,
a bucket, a duck, and me.

I am going to sleep with Violet
in Violet's race car bed,
on Violet's panda bear pillow.
"Good night, Hat," Violet said.

# The Song of Harvey's
## GALOSHES

When it's raining Harvey always puts us on,
  *puts us on,*
we're together when the sunny weather's gone,
  *weather's gone,*
O there's mud up to our tops,
we hope Harvey never stops
making deep, wet footprints in the lawn,
  *in the lawn.*

Squash-ga*losh*, squash-ga*losh*, through the slime,
Squash-ga*losh*, squash-ga*losh*, bet a nickel, bet a dime,

that the worms are squirming too,
for we wish to squish a few—
when it's raining don't we have a lovely time,
  *lovely time!*

# Emily's UNDIES

We're Emily's undies
with laces and bows.
Emily shows us
wherever she goes.
She doesn't wear diapers,
not even to bed.
Now she wears undies
with ruffles instead.

We're Emily's undies,
fit for a queen,
the prettiest undies
that anyone's seen,
and everyone's seen
our laces and bows
because Emily shows us
wherever she goes.

# Bob's
# BICYCLE HELMET

Bob's on his bike
and I'm on Bob.
I'm Bob's helmet.
I'm on the job.

Bob burns rubber.
Bob climbs hills.
Bob does wheelies.
Bob takes spills.

Bob skins his elbow.
Bob scrapes his knee.
Bob doesn't hurt his head—
Bob's got me.

And if some day
the sky should fall
it will not hurt
Bob's head at all.

Bob's on his bike again.
I'm on Bob.
I've got him covered.
I'm on the job.

# Jennifer's SHOES

We are Jennifer's shoes.
We came home in a box.
Now we go walking
when Jennifer walks.
When Jennifer walks,
we step out, too—
one of Jennifer's feet
per shoe.

We are learning the ways
of Jennifer's world:
the way that Jennifer's
toes are curled,
the softness of carpet,
the steepness of stair,
the curve of the rung
under Jennifer's chair,
the hole in the heel
of Jennifer's socks . . .

We are Jennifer's shoes,
we came home in a box.

# Joshua's JAMMIES

We are the jammies that Joshua wears,
    not jammies for penguins,
    not jammies for bears,
    not jammies for tigers with knots in their tails,
    not jammies for chickens,
    not jammies for whales,
    not jammies for elephants going upstairs,
we are the jammies that Joshua wears.
    We don't fit iguanas,
    we're not for the gnu,
    we won't suit the llamas
    (they never wear blue).
Hippopotamus can't get us over his head.
We're JOSHUA'S jammies. We're going to bed.

# Tanya's
## OLD T-SHIRT

I live in a bucket shoved under a stair.
They call me a *dust rag*!
I don't think it's fair.

I'm still the same size as when I was new.
*I* didn't shrink—
it was Tanya who **GREW**.

She started out small and we fit to a T.
Now she's big as a sofa!
She's tall as a tree!
*She's* out of control, and they're dusting with *me*!

You'll never, not *ever*
hear anyone say,
"She's gotten too big, she's just in the way,
let's dust the piano with Tanya today."

# Wanda's SWIMSUIT

We like to be wet,
Wanda and I,
I'm Wanda's swimsuit,
we don't like *dry*.

Ready, set, *jump!*
   Scrunch up small—
      *Look out down below—*

CANNONBALL!

Everybody dry
just got wetter.
(Wanda and I
think wetter is better.)

# Jack's SOCCER JERSEY

When Jack plays soccer we get our kicks.
I'm Jack's jersey.
I'm number **6**.

I show the number for me and Jack,
**6** in front
and **6** in back.

Jack does the running, I do the showing—
number **6** coming
number **6** going.

I show the number, Jack does the kicks.
I'm Jack's jersey—
Way to go **6**!

# Jamelia's
## DRESS-UP CLOTHES

Jamelia's playing dress-up
and we are playing, too—

Aunt Marina's swimsuit,
Cousin Bessie's shoes,
Mama's silk pajama tops,
Grandma's panty hose—

Jamelia wears us all at once.
We're her dress-up clothes.

# Rick's WOOL SWEATER

I'm Rick's wool sweater,
I make Rick twitchy—
wool feels itchy
next to his skin.

So it isn't any wonder he
wears a T-shirt under me:
warm on the OUTside
soft on the IN.

Still . . .

To tell the truth it tickles me
to be a little prickly,
especially around his neck
and under his chin.

# Clyde's COSTUME

I'm a gingham sheet and I used to sleep
tucked into the guest room bed.
One day—*surprise!* Clyde cut out eyes
and slipped me over his head.

Now I'm ghastly and ghoulish and ghostly,
a will-o'-the-wispy fright.
Pardon my pride, but with Clyde inside,
I'm the hit of Halloween night.

(There are other ghosts but mostly
the other ghosts are white.
I don't like to boast, but no other ghost
is gingham.)

# Hand-me-down SWEATSHIRT

I'm a hand-me-down sweatshirt
with zipper and hood.
I'm everyone's favorite
and still looking good.

I've been lost and recovered,
been torn and been sewn,
been dribbled on, tumbled in,
rained on and blown.

I started out Wendell's,
was passed down to May,
she passed me to Karly,
I'm Andrew's today.

So zip up my zipper
and pull up my hood.
I'm a friend of the family
and still looking good.

# Bill's **BLUE JACKET**

I'm Bill's blue jacket,
everybody cheer!
Bill's going to put me on—
Bill's right
*HERE!*

Bill's going to take me
off of the hook!
*Take me out! Shake me out!*
*How do I look?*

Arm in the left sleeve,
arm in the right.
*Button up! Button up! Button up*
*TIGHT!*

*Snap!* goes the collar
under Bill's chin.
Everybody holler,
*BILL'S ALL IN!*

Everybody clap your hands,
everybody shout,
*Bill's got his jacket on,*
*LET'S GO OUT!*

Alice Schertle is an award-winning poet whose books for children include *Little Blue Truck, Little Blue Truck Leads the Way, Very Hairy Bear,* and *All You Need for a Snowman.* She lives in Plainfield, Massachusetts, where she's all too familiar with buttoning up and trying to stay warm.

Petra Mathers has illustrated many gorgeous picture books, including *In Aunt Giraffe's Green Garden* by Jack Prelutsky, *The Miraculous Tale of the Two Maries* by Rosemary Wells, and her own Lottie series. She lives in Astoria, Oregon.